On the Soul & the Psyche

An Interactive Chapbook Exploring the Intersections of Introspective Expression

Daniel Cristina Figueroa

"I always speak the truth. Not the whole truth, because there's no way to say it all. Saying it all is literally impossible: words fail. Yet it's through this very impossibility that the truth holds onto the real."

Jacques Lacan, *Télévision* 1973

CONTENTS

feel free to draw in this book as you please

what else are margins for?

6

FOREWORD

This interactive chapbook invites you to an
experience of self-discovery.
You do not have to be an artist or a poet to
express your emotions.
What you do not want to say aloud can be
drawn or written.
My goal is to inspire you to let go of
what you were taught to
hold in.
Write, draw, and reflect as you see fit.

Life Cycles

In conversation with "Poem" by Muriel Rukeyser

I lived through crimes against humanity and nature

junior year of high school, in U.S. History class, postponing
coursework,
completely powerless, witnessing a race for power
people spoke words of praise and empathy in support,
ignorant to what was in store:
the winner—uneducated, prejudiced, villainous
revoking people's dreams with the family, the house, and the
white picket fence,
while the bystanders get quieter and quieter,
until they're kneeling in silence,
but even that's too loud for society to bear.

recalling the debate of the world's end,
resulting in either fire or ice,
Frost believed that either would suffice, yet
I'm leaning toward fire, as we lose sight of the densest ice
we watch the wind whirl in different directions,
convincing us that the seasons are simply indecisive
news reports of shell casings falling from the sky,
not very close to me but close to us
crimes against humanity
that we've only heard about in history,
resurfacing as if time is cyclical

I lived through the world as we know it; slipping through our
fingertips.

What states of the world
have you lived through?

How have they affected the
world today?

_____
_____
_____
_____
_____
_____
_____
_____
_____
_____
_____
_____
_____
_____
_____
_____
_____
_____
_____
_____
_____

[shit] we just don't talk about

if poetry is what he/she/they thought
but didn't say[1] ,

what she said was:
"she got herself into it and
she can get herself out"

                      what she thought was:

but she did not say,
nor did he,
nor did they.

after they hung up the phone
I felt poems rushing
down my face,
my voice trembled, alone.

---

[1] Adapted from Heather McHugh's "What He Thought" 1994

how could I love them
when they fed
into [shit] that
"we just don't talk about?"

I wonder if they'll hear
the years-worth of tears
I shed for them,
they told me to
hold.

Have you ever been told not to talk about something?
Maybe something others have overcompensated for?
How has it affected you or those around you?

Draw yourself saying something you were told not to talk about

Draw yourself
here:

Try to fill the speech bubble as much as you can

Other things I have been told not to talk abou

aftermath of [unconditional] love

they told me to hold my tongue
as if I would listen,
surprisingly articulate
through the heavy breathing,
and tremors of frustration,

as if her life depended
on my voice.

the aftermath of this [event],
was loss of faith
and trust in my family.

four of us raised together,
and I believed our bond
was stronger than the links
of a metal chain.

[shit] was always a game of
monkey-see-monkey-do,
I saw them but
they never truly saw me.

reason, honesty,
and authenticity,

I watched them fall
victim to the opposite,
and I refused to play.

the aftermath was resentment
toward those who have expressed
the notion of unconditional love,
those who have taught me
that mine is not.

how could I
when they fed
into [shit] that
"we just don't talk about?"

youngest of the four
but I never stopped trying
to save them from
themselves and
the history they saw as fate,

from the stories our mothers told us
about the violent fluctuations
of their lives

and the lessons they learned
the hard way,
without the time to play games.

the aftermath is
the distance [shit] put between us
the distance kept between us

as I wish they heard my voice
through the tin-can telephone
rolling the tongue
they told me
to hold.

What does unconditional love mean to you?

_____
_____
_____
_____
_____
_____
_____
_____
_____
_____
_____
_____
_____
_____
_____
_____
_____
_____
_____
_____
_____
_____

Conditions of my love:

on the soul

I

constantly seeking to fuel an endless fire
foolishly connecting the stars in the sky
wishing upon a map of our desires
maybe He will answer if we try

the essence of life, energy and power,
nestled deep inside of us,
the uncharted element we're denied
the fifth—the purest
permeating the celestial sphere,
this is my first theory
I have yet to search everywhere

II

I never lose the thought of you,
your face never leaves my mind
I don't write about you often,
but I talk to you in His house
all the time

I wish I could've told you how much
your presence meant to me
the absence never goes unnoticed;
you're no longer napping in your bedroom
or sitting on the couch humming
only pictures on every screen and wall.

missing you feels selfish
because of how I am reminded of your soul,
its unburdened freedom
relieved from the pain of its vessel.

> you were in the hospital for two weeks
> with no hope of rehabilitation
> well enough to FaceTime me but you couldn't speak
> yet your eyes registered my face without complication
> when I arrived, I sat with you
> until I could no longer contain it

so instead,
I imagine your Heaven,
where pain doesn't exist, and the mind no longer plays tricks:

your boat docked off the coast of San Juan,
singing "vamos a la playa,"
you go there everyday
fishing pole in hand,
you walk out of your small house and onto the beach
then fish for a few hours until there's enough for dinner.

when the sun sets, you walk back home,
sit on the couch,
pick up a quarter and
resume the scratch-off lottery ticket from earlier that day.

each time you finish one, another one appears on the table,
next to your coffee mug and glazed stick donut.
after a shower comes a nap,
there are no kids here to disturb you.

> our generation gap put a barrier of language between us
> but we never allowed it to take its toll
> communicating through what we did know
> and non-verbal conversations
> now every time I run on Dunkin'
> I can't leave without a glazed stick donut
> regardless of my location,
> my forever ode to you.

III

resurrection day—
the most popular day to talk to Him.
we walked back to the pew from receiving communion,
kneeled, bowed our heads and closed our eyes,
hopeful that He opens his ears to our prayers.

> our lack of consistency led us
> to delve into our deepest selves,
> pulling on the strings
> tugging on them one by one,
> invoking emotions that we only confront in our solitude.

my mother rarely cried alone,
her emotions,
equipped with the strength to evoke my own.
unable to read each other's minds
nor hear each other's prayers,
it only takes an exchange of looks for me to know,
merging streams.

> without a word, I leaned over to hug her
> then we resumed our seats
> and attempted to internalize the rest
> I held her hand until it was time to leave.

the words of the priest,
submerged beyond the realm of thought,
playing from a boombox outside the window to the soul.

> I know she was thinking of you,
> of your soul,
> and how she held your hand until it decided to go.
> if she wonders where you are,
> I'll tell her you're one with the fifth element,
> her North Star.

somehow, I'm still tempted to ask Him:
how do we feed this force that is unable to communicate contentment?
does it reject us when we are not tasteful?
will it live on without us?

What comes to your mind
when you consider the soul?

What does it mean to you?

siren song on vinyl

where every note sounds the same
aching for a new voice,
resting at the sound of your name,

my internal melodies
never seem to remedy
the siren song inside of me.

in my solitude the needle pirouettes across
the modulated vinyl grooves
and over divots of emotion

it's more mezzo-soprano
no, alto
actually bass.

I watch as the
rapids rush over rocks
pushing against a dam

that continues to amplify,
                barricaded
between *o v e r l a p p i n g   w   a   v   e   s.*

you tried and tried to find
the song inside,
rattling

—a door in duress
then I heard the record scratch.
why wouldn't it play for you?

breathe in and out,
with the smoke
you see as a mask

self-inflicted
as if I picked up a paintbrush
and spun the wheel

—a new color every day,
red and orange on friday
blue and pink on monday and

purple on saturday
just for *you,*
although none ring true.

the paint drips down my cheek
forming a barrier between the needle
                              and the record
held open by a force like Atlas,

burdened by past mistakes
that I carry in my eyes unwillingly,
just as he bears them on his back.

—an ocean of melodies
I try to differentiate between
the deep blue *o v e r l a p p i n g   w a v e s*

as time elapsed,
the scratch began to fade and
I felt the song change.

I took a deep breath in,
and out through my mouth,
swaddled by the *o v e r l a p p i n g   w a v e s*

searching for the melodies calling me.

Create a metaphor for how you feel
when you are overwhelmed.

A metaphor is, by definition:
a comparison of two things without using
like or as

For example: When I am happy I shine
brighter than the sun
or my pillow is a soft cloud

Reconciliation

she said it feels like the trees are breathing
the leaves bleeding orange into red
one would usually sense danger
when eyes glow and curls turn into snakes
only one number on the door, seven
forgot to knock and now she's stripping

knocked so hard the paint was stripping
running so fast, I was barely breathing
I only needed one mile but that was seven
it's so cold my nose and ears are red
my foot got caught in a hose, not strangling snakes
the cold wind alleviated my thoughts of danger

dreams induce a false impression of danger
watching faces melt with skin stripping
no eyes, just snakes
hissing and heavy breathing
overhead lights glowing bright red
I recognize their faces, a total of seven

she said "baby it's not that much, only seven"
overwhelming love means danger
gripping thorns turning the rose from white to red
regifting with no intention of stripping
chest to chest, in sync, breathing
infatuation that'll swallow you whole like snakes

 swift movements, stealthy as snakes
the breaking news on channel seven
after the bite she stopped breathing
she didn't think she was in danger
her memory is stripping
eyes—bloodshot red

she bought it because my favorite color is red
her name wrapped around my mind like intertwining snakes
now it makes me cringe like the sound of floorboards stripping
I fought each sin, all seven
seeking reconciliation rather than danger
sun rays dance through the stained glass, colors breathing

yellow, blue and green stripping until the truth shone red
confessions through intervals of breathing, speaking in the tongue of snakes
watching the sign as seven butterflies swarm, beauty and affection masking danger.

What is something
you've reconciled with--or
hope to?

what color does your truth shine?

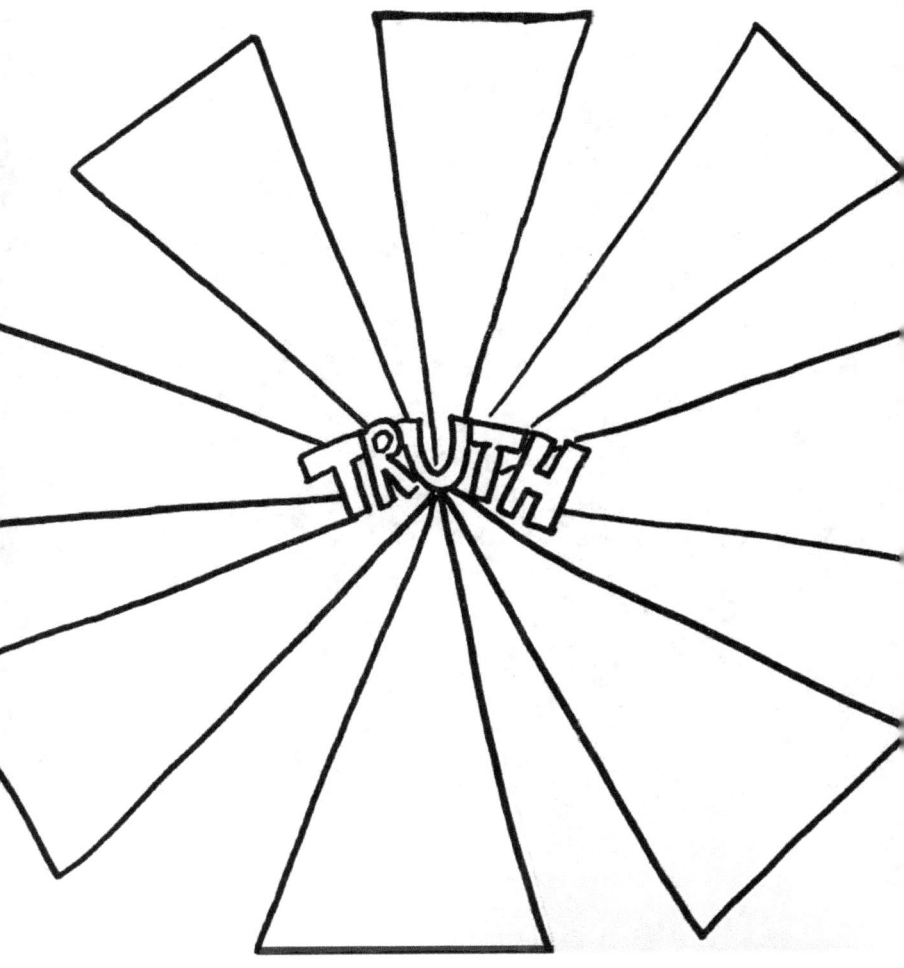

fill the outline with colors of your choice

why my heart has renamed itself *Commitment Issues:*

bc it's untrustworthy
unreliable
careless
truly unpredictable

bc my emotions fluctuate
like a r o l l e r c o a s t e r
upside-down &
under the tunnel
shit makes me dizzy

bc i search for answers
but they get lost in the tension
w/ my desires
that i struggle to constellate

bc i'm never satisfied
everyone is missing something
& exceeds where the other lacks

bc my body should not
be equipped to hand out pleasure
like Oprah hands out cars

tainting the fantasies of men
who believe they should be praised
like kings

entrenched in their desire to enact them
always willing to pull out
a ring

or lock hips mid-thrust
emphasizing
the question of trust

encircling the temple to worship me in
different ways
different languages
different motions

constantly seeking my attention
my affection
slowly
i felt the warmth of passion
on one corner
in attempt to melt the ice
around *Commitment Issues*

i don't burn sage to purify the air
i'd rather roll something stronger
to nullify the negativity
i try to keep buried

but sometimes creeps
through the roots &

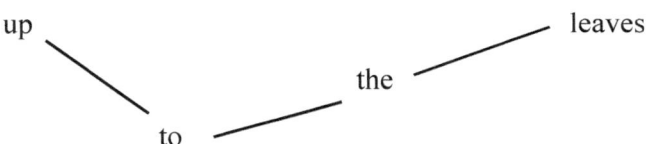

infecting how
they seed me

i tend to misread
the ripeness of relations
prematurity is malignant in itself

there's no peacetime in my mind
so i search for the white flag
stars flash as if they're waving

bc *Commitment Issues*
blames everything
on the scorpio in me

asked if i see it
crawling under my skin
or hear its whisper
in the back of my head
when i face
my "intense" passion for
authenticity
real intimacy
& the truth of course
but that's just according to my ego
apparently
the moon controls my inner tides
and my emotional self is repressed

i have no comeback for this.

in the light of venus
i'm idealistic
eager to please
willing to compromise
yet self-obsessed
and struggle with being
loyal

venus is in the fifth house
implying i express love
through self-expression
creativity
& pleasure
my hair hides my eyes yet
the stars try to recognize
the mask i wear
the ascendant
the bull with its horns
apparently attuned to pleasure
grounded to the earth
but my thoughts are subdued by water

i shouldn't blame the stars for a life
dictated by pleasure
i blame myself

i can only run in my dreams
i can never fight
unequipped with the sting of a scorpion
the strength of the bull
must weigh
down my hand and

instill the

    s l o w e s t m o t i o n   e v e r

i scream in objection
as they denounce it in public:

guilty of empty promises
guarded by teeth with no bite

      Commitment Issues in the guillotine
            my mind
        the executioner.

My sun sign is:

My moon sign is:

rising

My rising (or ascendant) sign is:

Do you know your astrological birth chart?
Google search a birth chart website or download
the Costar app to your phone.
You'll need the time, date, and location of your
birth. Make note of what your signs are and the
characteristics associated with them.

Do you believe in astrology?
Was knowing your chart helpful to you?
What do your astrological
signs suggest about you?
Do you think they're true/correct?
What do you blame for your habits/ tendencies?
Do you fight them?

DANIELA C. FIGUEROA

the temple

some tried to knock
some looked for the bell

they tried to caress cold-
blooded claws to avoid
being stung with the
poison

oh, the poison!
toxically sweet

sweeter than
ripe pineapple
the taste still sweet
on your lips dripping

down your hips
pounding
but you're not inside
numb overwhelmed
by lust temptation

few made it in,
it's forbidden to
stay.

the temple of: _____

_____
_____
_____
_____
_____
_____
_____
_____
_____
_____
_____
_____
_____
_____
_____
_____
_____
_____
_____
_____
_____
_____
_____
_____
_____
_____
_____

If you consider your body as a temple, what would it look like? What would be inside it? Who would be allowed in?

velvet tension

love is life's VIP section
cut off by velvet ropes,

crowded with bottle girls
pouring champagne
as the dance floor falls silent.

it was lust,
not love.

mesmerized by sparklers
and speaker vibrations
I watch in envy

the sound of silence
never sounded so clear.

I learned that silence
could hold you,
comfort you
and whisper truth

to thrive beyond those ropes
is to be immersed in emotional
commotion

caught in the velvet tension
between lust and love,

and if I stay very still I might
feel the velvet
drawn before my eyes
as I sit on the dancefloor
in complete silence.

Have you ever felt torn between love and lust? What do these terms mean to you?

What is your velvet tension?

Draw your head under the thought bubble and fill the thought bubble with your velvet tension

violin song

I woke up to the sweetest song
I wondered where it was coming from

I looked out my window and
began to watch in awe

as she played her violin
my watching forbidden,
it felt like a sin.

it was the sweetest song
I've ever heard
full of lust or mistrust.

watching,
listening
to the song resonate

from her heart strings
as if a violin.

but where was the bow?
my hand fell to the floor

there it was.
my chest began to feel sore
never felt hollow as a violin before

I woke to the sweetest song
stuck in my head

playing over and over
because I played her
just like a violin.

What kind of song best defines
your past or present relationship?
What genre would it be?
What instruments would it use?
Where would it come from?

[self acceptance] guided poem

Fill in the blanks with your thoughts regarding
self-acceptance.
Feel free to add to or change the phrases as you see fit.

Some guiding questions to consider are:

°   what does self-acceptance mean to you?

°   have you struggled with it?

°   what advice would you give yourself or someone else?

Start with a simile:

self-acceptance is like

it seems easy but

I would define it as

it can look like

I have accepted that I

I can be more accepting of myself by

[rewrite your poem as you see fit]

Title: _____

use this side for more writing or drawing

I don't want to write about COVID (2020-2021)

when the real pandemic
is hate
& ignorance the plague

in their minds
spread by mouth and
social media

and I don't want to
be home all the time
but I want to be
safe, & keep my friends and family safe

wondering why
things haven't changed
when they shouldn't have
been that way
in the first place

deep rooted
history sprouted from the bullshit

"...as violence continues to plague American cities"
the newscaster says.

my cousin moved to Kentucky
running from her baby daddy

caught him
"lackin'" leaving a store
isn't the gun
a coward's weapon?

...as if this is reality?

when her sister asked
what I've been doing
because I look "thick"
and i didn't have the answers
she was looking for
happy, healthy post quarantine body

all hunkered down
but I've never felt further
I offer my ears or just my arms
but both are denied

when we're immersed
in a social world drenched
in interaction and now

we must keep our distance

when the wind blew over my mirror
and it shattered
so, I tried to coax my mind to
not be superstitious

with unemployment
out the ass

companies hiring
but not really hiring

the most significant economic shock
since the Great Depression [1]

while we're struggling
to plan forward, too busy fixing
remnants of the past

the "new normal"
but this shit will never be normal

---

1 https://www.bbc.com/news/science-environment-55498657

while we're going
through the motions
trying to regain sight of reality
with the tickle

of a q-tip in your nose
the new social hour
as we cheer each other on
praising the booger swab

with heightened emotions
because life never stopped
cities and towns reopening

but life always finds a way in,
invited itself
(without a mask)

while minds sicker
than the virus
are constantly trying

to whisper
threatening fantasies
deadlier than 45's "cure"
his followers blind

he finessed his way
to the top
of the game,

that's all he sees
as if we're chess pieces
on a board

a game he doesn't even understand

and Kanye can't even
explain, he used to love himself
the most
but he's losing sight
all he sees is 45s

and his wife*,
after (14) years their
clout is fading
oh, what a tragedy!

that no one really cares.

because we need to protect our girls
from the media

where they're encouraged
to exploit themselves

even if it's in French
@Netflix

shit, it's the W.A.P. era
but that's not the intention

female rappers coming for the men
that sexualize them 24/7

but a woman shouldn't speak like that, right?

when SNL's Senator Harris
proudly said we need a W.A.P.,
a "woman as president"

regardless of what we say,
we would be more articulate than 45
in the 2020 debate

because it's heartbreaking,
truly upsetting

other countries
laughing

while we watch,
with fear in our eyes

because the violence
seems to never end

because the news
said the rise in violence
is due to the stress
of YOU

is that why
Tory shot Meg?

is that why
those "cops"

shot Jacob Blake?
and Breonna Taylor?

when the climate is **still**
changing and California is **still**
on fire

because **when will this end**?

do we have to burn it **all**
down and start over?

we'd probably be free of you
if it wasn't for 45's supporters
but no,
they were too busy storming
the U.S. Capitol

literally scaling the walls
breaking in,
entering offices of Senators and
Congress members

but you know the story—
(January 6, 2021)

because they call this
the land of the free
but who exactly is free?

because they arrest
BLM protesters
but 45 supporters
get the royal treatment

when we've been inside for so long
*the KimYe era has ended

we try our best to go out but
it's cold outside,
the snow is beginning to melt
next week it'll be warm
then comes all the rain

because two weeks ago
it snowed in every county in Texas
for the first time in over 100 years
yes, snow in Texas

because...

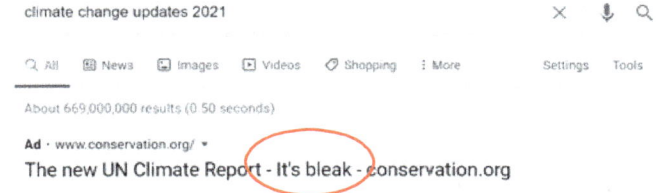

but at least,
they've created multiple
vaccinations
the only hope we
have to hold
each other's hands
in search of some
form of "new" peace

because I'm in the middle
of planning for the future
yet you're indefinitely, unwillingly
lurking through the timeline

I'd rather go back
to 2006

and hit the rewind button
like Adam Sandler in "Click"

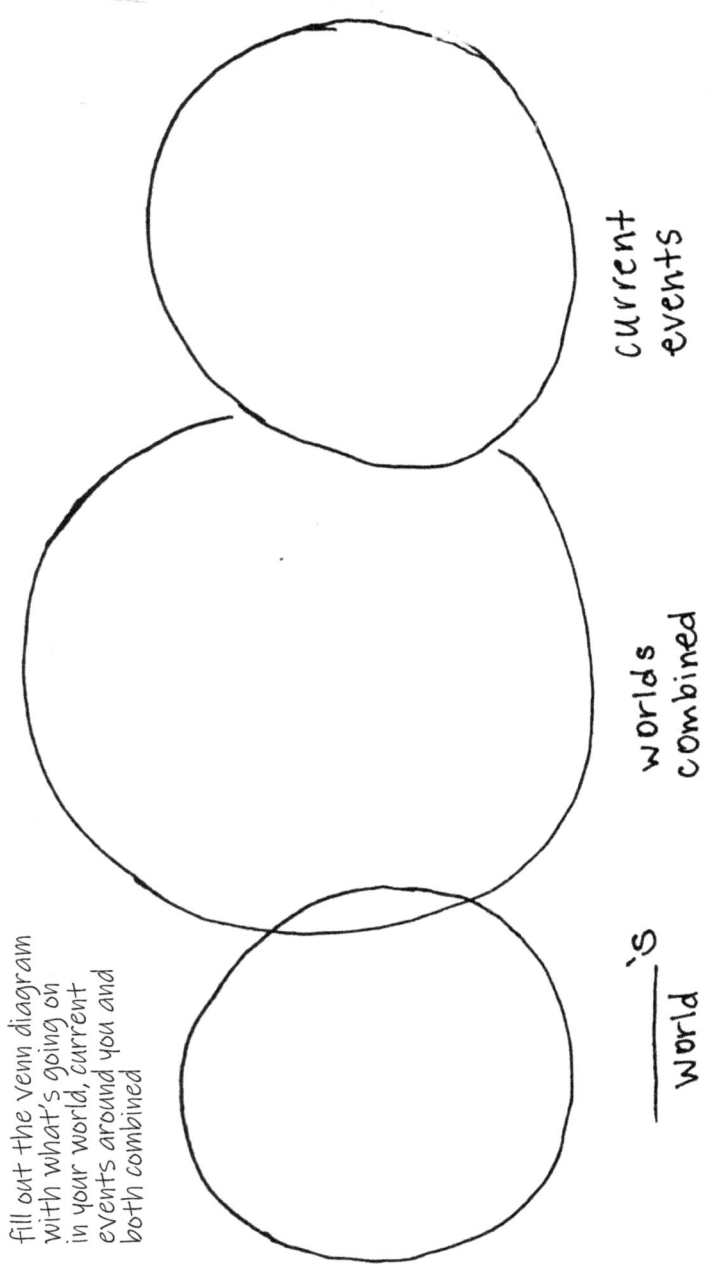

current events

worlds combined

_____'s world

fill out the venn diagram with what's going on in your world, current events around you and both combined

Consider things that have happened in your life and things that have happened on a worldwide scale. Write about them together.

Example: personal life, COVID-19 and news/ media around the same time

WARNING

will my mind ever rest
not toss and turn until thoughts have faded?
in my head I must make my own peace
and play the song stuck in there out loud
running out but do I even care?
my heart split like a pomegranate

huddled like seeds of a pomegranate
in this safe space—your shoulder a headrest
it's a part of our self care
rolling down hills of emotion until side effects have faded
turning heads because this pack is always loud
as we walk toward peace

the constant presence of hate delays peace
blinded, red, eyes bleeding the shade of pomegranate
when the country mourns, it screams aloud
orange is sus', it's himself he should arrest
his future on top faded
who knows if he ever cared

we keep rolling to ease life's scare
hoping we achieve some peace
but time is running out, the hourglass faded
blood spilt thicker than the juice of a pomegranate
the hands of injustice laying our souls to rest
their last cries echo, resonating aloud

there's no cure, the only treatment is loud
unnecessary criminalization will change if they start to care
it's legal almost everywhere, some places are the unfairest
if we start with each other, come together piece by piece
we'll find it as easy as eating a pomegranate
but until then we'll be getting faded

true colors can hide and appear faded
but under pressure they're quite loud
lips stained after eating a pomegranate
blood-stained hands without a care
listen, all of us screaming for peace
through the smoke is when we see clearest

warning papers from my tight circle like a pomegranate, only 5 but we've
been there many times it's fated
sealed with the PURE HEMP crest, the only way to roll loud
care or don't care, this isn't a wake-up call it's a WARNING—peace

How do you relieve your stress?
Do you cope or indulge?
How can you be more mindful
in moments of indulgence?

use this entire page to create a collage utilizing images (from magazines, newspapers, pictures, drawings, etc.) that show how you practice self-care

FULL PAINTINGS

Life Cycles
acrylic on canvas
16x20in.

aftermath of [unconditional] love
acrylic on canvas
with digital photo overlaid
8x10in.

on the soul
acrylic on canvas
16x20in.

siren song on vinyl
acrylic on canvas
16x20in.

Reconciliation
acrylic on canvas
18x24in.

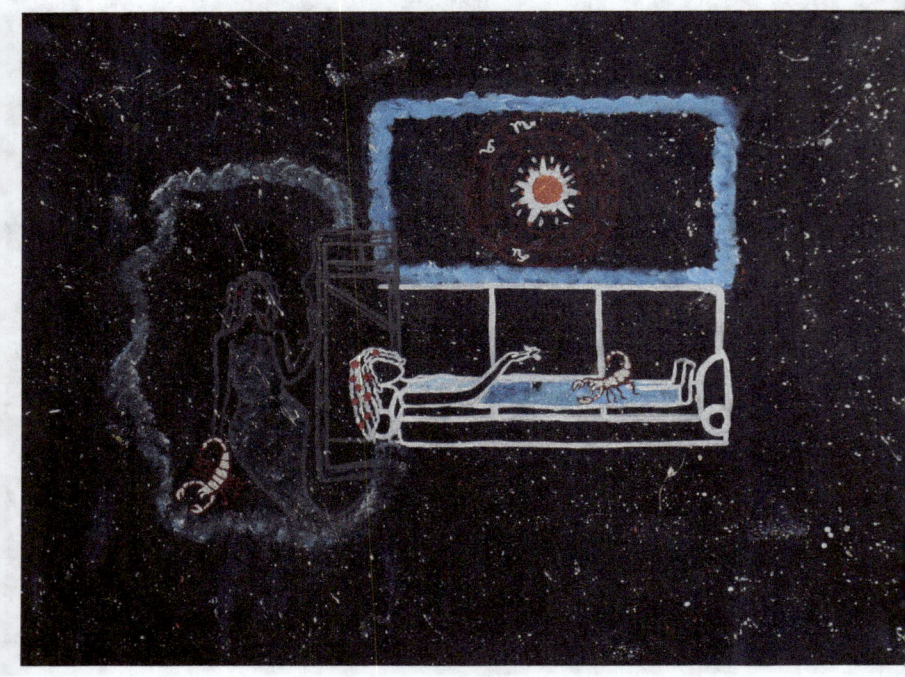

why my heart has renamed itself Commitment Issues
acrylic on canvas
18x24in.

the temple
acrylic on canvas
16x20in. oval

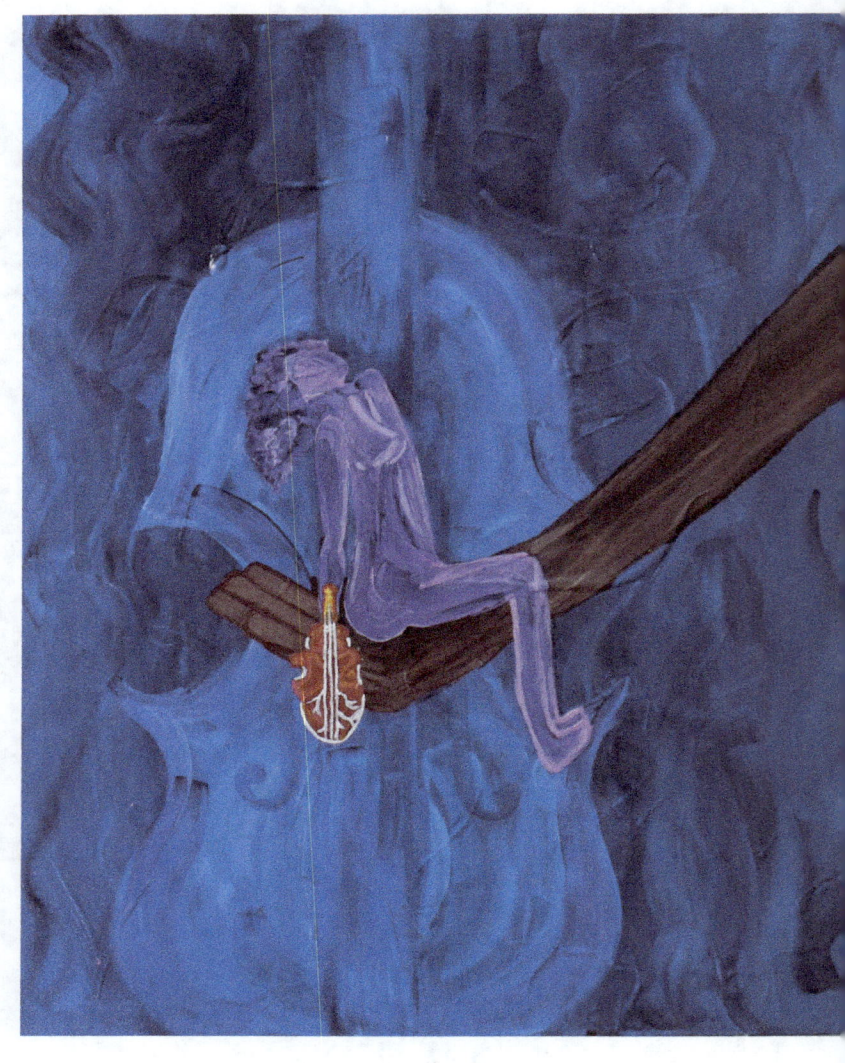

violin song
acrylic on canvas panel
16x20in.

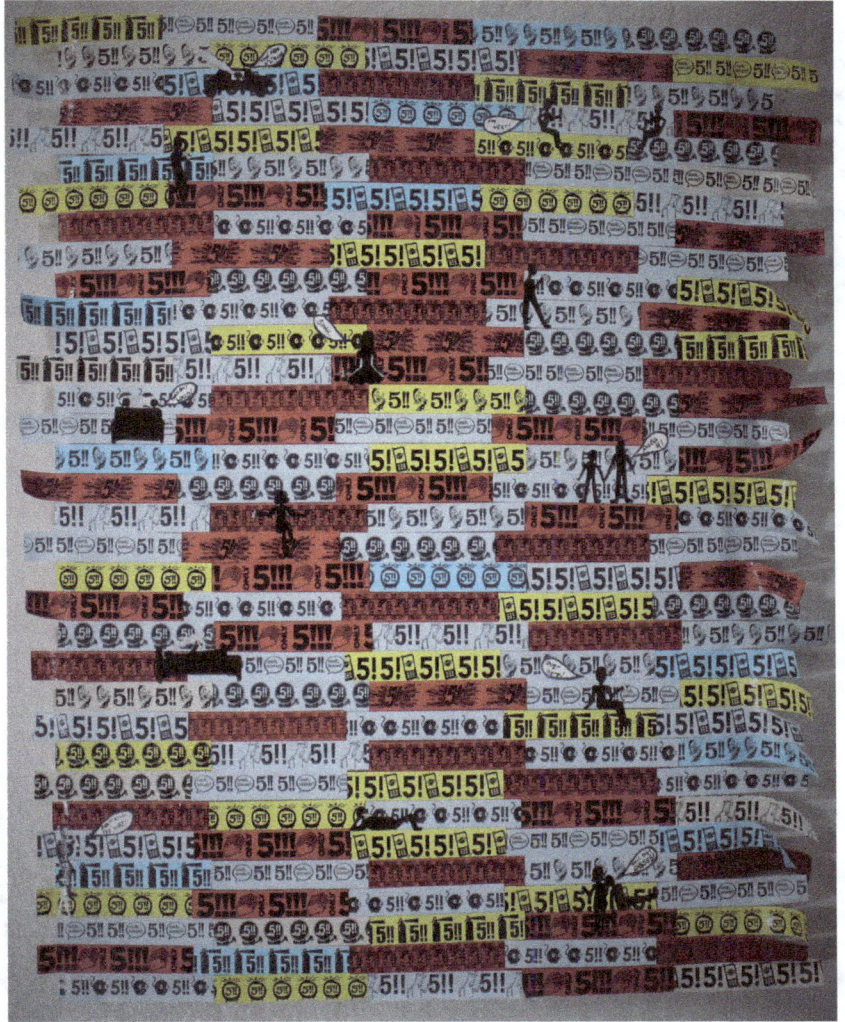

WARNING
acrylic paint,
'warning' papers
(from Bob Marley Pure Hemp rolling papers)
18x24in. canvas

WARNING
close ups

AFTERWORD

In 2017, I wrote my college essay about someone I called Amaranthine Vitality. She was my chosen mask—a figment of my mind that lived in the realm of my short stories and poetry. With fire and immortality in her arsenal she was undefeated, fearless yet bore the weight of emotions. She fought with a heavy heart that was guarded by gilded armor. I wanted to hide behind her resilience.

I never thought she would shed a tear. I didn't want her to. Signing off on repressing emotions with a capital A.V.. I knew it was wrong, so I had to save myself from the universe of my mind. Free myself from my vision of her to create the vision of me: one who is not afraid to feel and defend those feelings, to myself and everyone who refuses to listen; one who is at peace with herself, who I am, and confidence in who I desire to be. I am not perfect, and I have no desire to be. I only want to be at peace and completely in love with me.

Thank you for joining me on my journey that's slightly incomplete.

I hope it inspires you to express yourself and discover more about yourself, in a way that is liberating.

Above all, your most important relationship is with yourself.

I wanted to create a chapbook exploring introspective (self) expression, and I never imagined it would evolve into this.

Originally, I wanted to share the results of my journey of learning how to express myself and finding my voice, yet I felt it would be pointless, if I didn't also invite others to engage in their own. I hoped to construct an experience that encourages the reader to explore the freedom of self-expression and the benefit of self-discovery through writing and creating art imbued with thoughts and emotions.

I wanted to include a direct invitation to the reader to engage with the content as much as possible because I never wrote in my books, even when I owned them.
In fear of "disrespecting" the authors work with my own thoughts or drawings. But I have come to learn that it's an essential part of the process of understanding and engaging.

This interactive chapbook was created as my undergraduate thesis project, as a result of my Division III (final year) at Hampshire College. This collection evolved over my four years at Hampshire and engages with my experiences during my journey of learning how to express myself, my perspectives and my identities.

The intersection of my psychoanalytic studies that coincides with my work mainly derives from Lacan's theory and discussion of what he calls "the Thing," and for Freud, "das Ding." My interpretation of this concept is that it's our truest and deepest unconscious desires, which cannot be attained, yet can be encircled and approached through associations and connections from objects that we establish and create (including visual art and poetry). It's this approach, this encircling, this desire—that acts as a catalyst for itself ensuring that we continue to desire. "-it being understood that, to a certain extent, a work of art always involves encircling the Thing" (*The Seminar of Jacques Lacan* Book VII).

Therefore, I genuinely believe our unconscious desires are inevitably imbued within visual art and poetry and can be used as a tool for introspective expression and self-discovery. Some would say the soul and the psyche are one in the same, my chapbook proves I beg to differ.

After all,

Where do you go when you want to look inside?
How can we access our *unconscious* thoughts and desires?
When language fails, how do we communicate?
Why do we *crave* interpretation?
How are emotions and messages conveyed within
paintings and poetry?
What are the *consequences* of their juxtaposition?
How does it make you feel?
Can I paint you a *metaphor*?
Can I write the colors of my thoughts?
Can I show and tell you *why?*
Why all I have is questions.
Why I am always *looking* for answers.
One brush stroke and letter at a time,
I am *finding* my answers.
But don't ask me what they are,
I want to *inspire* you to find yours.
I began with exploring ways to efficiently
express my suppressed *thoughts* and *emotions.*
Now I say "*acrylic on canvas.*"
I hope that my work will encourage others,
especially other young women to *express* themselves.
Regardless of the topic, your thoughts are meaningful.
Don't hold your tongue. Let it go. Write about it.
Make them *see* you. Make them *hear* you.

ACKNOWLEDGEMENTS

I would like to thank my Hampshire College advising committee, Nathan McClain and John Slepian for their guidance and support. I'm appreciative of Nathan for witnessing my poetry grow over the past few years, providing me with the knowledge to push them further and evidently allowing me to prove to myself that I have a lot more to say than I ever would have imagined.

I would also like to thank my former advisor Annie Rogers, for her teachings of psychoanalysis that have resonated within my work ever since.

Huge shout-out to my siblings and friends, my fellow pomegranate seeds for their endless support and encouragement.

Most importantly, this wouldn't have been possible without the support of my parents who I am eternally grateful for.

& thank *you*, for staying with me until the end.

Journaling Tips

1st: I like to add the date and exact time to my journal
(I think it's interesting to look back on)

2nd: when I start to write I like to consider:

- what's going on in my life?

- what's going on in the world around me?

- how do those things make me feel and what are my opinions on them?

- observations I've made that stuck with me--even an observation about myself
(ex. attitude/emotions)

- what's currently on my mind? writing it out allows me to think through what's going on

- a phrase or idea that I find interesting

- an image that inspires an idea
(ekphrastic poetry)

- anything is meaningful if it resonates with you

3rd: I doodle any images that come to mind
while writing

Use the extra lined pages to
expand on prompts or
begin to practice journaling on
your own.

time for a new journal, you got this!